HOW TO REVIEW TAX RETURNS

Edward Mendlowitz, CPA

Andrew D. Mendlowitz

Published by CPA Trendlines
Actionable intelligence for the tax, accounting and finance community
cpatrendlines.com

Library Data

Mendlowitz, Edward; and Mendlowitz, Andrew D.
How to Review Tax Returns
ISBN-13: 978-0991266203
ISBN-10: 099126620X
1. Accounting firms – Management. 2. Accounting firms – United States
I. Mendlowitz, Edward, 1942-
and Mendlowitz, Andrew D., 1973 -

CONTENTS

About the Authors

Edward Mendlowitz

Ed Mendlowitz is a partner in the New Brunswick, N.J., office of WithumSmith+Brown, PC, and has more than 40 years of public accounting experience. He is a licensed certified public accountant in the states of New Jersey and New York and is accredited by the American Institute of Certified Public Accountants (AICPA) in business valuation (ABV), certified in financial forensics (CFF) and as a personal financial specialist (PFS). He also has the AICPA CITP and CGMA designations. Ed is also admitted to practice before the United States Tax Court and has testified as an expert witness in federal and state court regarding business valuations, and before the House Ways and Means Committee on Tax Equity, Reform and Reduction.

A graduate of City College of New York, Ed earned his bachelor of business administration degree. He is a member of the AICPA, the New Jersey Society of Certified Public Accountants (NJSCPA) and the New York State Society of Certified Public Accountants (NYSSCPA). In addition, Ed was a founding partner of Mendlowitz Weitsen, LLP, CPAs which merged with WS+B in 2005. Currently, he serves on the NYSSCPA Estate Planning Committee, and was chairman of the committee that planned the NYSSCPA's 100th anniversary. The author of over 20 books, Ed has also written hundreds of articles for business and professional journals and newsletters. He is a contributing editor to the Practitioners Publishing Company's 1998/1999 *706/709 Deskbook*, and various and current editions of Wiley's *Handbook on Budgeting, Corporate Controller's Handbook* and the AICPA *Management of an Accounting Practice Handbook* and is on the editorial board of *Bottom Line/Personal* newsletter. Appearing regularly on television news programs, Ed has also been quoted in many major newspapers and periodicals in the United States. He is the recipient of the Lawler Award for the best article published during 2001 in the *Journal of Accountancy*.

Ed is a frequent speaker to many professional and business groups, including the AICPA, NJSCPA, NYSSCPA, American Management Association, the National Committee for Monetary Reform, University of Medicine and Dentistry in N.J. and many more. For 11 years, he taught courses on financial analysis, corporate financial policy and theory, monetary and fiscal policy and financial and managerial accounting in the MBA program at Fairleigh Dickinson University.

Andrew D. Mendlowitz

Andrew is an award winning journalist and author of the book, *Ireland's Professional Amateurs*. He is a graduate of the University of Maryland with a degree in journalism. He started his career while still a college student with over 250 freelance articles appearing in the Washington Post. Presently he works on contract writing assignments.

Acknowledgements

This book is based on my lifelong professional quest to develop methods that work. It is also the result of long term collaboration with clients, partners, staff and colleagues in a combined journey to be more effective and have more effective assistants and co-workers.

It is impossible to acknowledge every contributor, simply because I am unable to call up from the recesses of my brain everyone that gave me an idea or thread that has been woven into the fabric of my methods.

However, there are many that clearly come to mind and they include my partners Peter A. Weitsen, Frank R. Boutillette, William Hagaman, Jr., John Mortenson, Dave Springsteen, Ron Bleich, Ruben Cardona, Howard Stein and Shree Nadkarni.

Others include Kevin Fellin, Mary Jane Younghans, Joe Picone, Brian Lovett, Debra Schmelzer, Michael Slotopolsky, Scott Perlzweig, Martin Abo, E. Martin Davidoff, Robbin Weiner and my former partners, Seymour G. Siegel and Paul H. Rich.

Thanks to Rick Telberg for publishing this book which contains procedures I know has helped thousands of CPA firms in having a better and more profitable and pleasant tax season.

This book primarily was written and organized by my son, Andy, from an unbelievable array of notes, speech handouts, and PowerPoint presentations I dumped on his desk or into his computer. Not being an accountant gave him practical insights to question me on procedures I assumed were common knowledge and for which he turned into a coherent and cohesive book. It was amazing to me how someone without any CPA firm experience could grasp the concepts and make them easily readable.

Some of the material in this book was adapted from *Managing Your Tax Season, Second Edition*, published by the AICPA, and I thank them for their permission to include it in here.

Everything I do, including this book, is done with the needed support and love of my wife Ronnie.

Foreword

Ed and I have been partners for 25 years. When we founded our firm I was designated the Tax Partner and Ed was the "Everything Else" Partner. One of my primary responsibilities was to be the reviewer of all of the firm's tax returns. Most of what I have learned over the years about the quality of tax returns comes from Ed.

A quote from Ed that I have heard many times over the years is that "When a client receives his or her tax return, at that moment it is the single most important thing on the client's mind." In fact the tax return may be the only tangible product that a client ever receives from an accounting firm. The return had better be right and presented professionally in an appealing package. (Ed once bought me a spool of blue ribbon to tie around the tax return folder we sent to clients, but in the heat of tax season I decided that I couldn't properly tie the bow.)

In the beginning I observed Ed filling in numbers on pre-printed four column accounting paper with his Cross pencil doing tax projections and tax comparisons of finished returns. My initial reaction was that this was crazy and probably a waste of time. Boy, I have surely changed my tune, especially now that it is done with computers and Excel software. More importantly this is a vital step in the tax review process as he explains inside this book.

One evening a few days before April 15, Ed was ready to send out the tax return of our richest client. It was quite involved and probably at least 100 pages. He asked me to flip through the pages to see if I could notice anything that could be an error or a red flag that would be picked up by the IRS. I found something! This then became a required tax review technique at our firm. Years later Ed and our new partner, Frank Boutillette, encouraged (actually forced) me to do two things – close my door for an hour and a half early in the morning and do the same shortly after we returned from lunch. This was to allow me to fully focus and devote uninterrupted time to the review of tax returns. You see, there were a number of preparers feeding returns to a single reviewer (me) and that was causing a log jam in getting returns out the door.

The other request was to review the returns on screen (now that I have a second monitor) rather than looking at printed pages before the return was final. Both of these "suggestions" worked tremendously and resulted in a higher and more efficient performance level and a better service to the client. In this book Ed is offering original ideas and sage advice about the entire tax return process. Read it closely and adapt it to your practice. You will be happier, more relaxed and richer for doing so.

Peter A. Weitsen, CPA, PFS
Partner, WithumSmith+Brown, PC

Facts, Conclusion and Mission

Fact: There are more preparers than reviewers.

Fact: Most preparers are at a lower level of expertise than reviewers.

Fact: If a bottleneck is going to develop it will be at the reviewer level.

Fact: Tax season is usually much busier than the rest of the year and can be very hectic.

Fact: Processes need to be established that will create uniformity of work and reduce review time, while increasing quality.

Fact: The reviewer is the guardian of the tax returns' quality.

Conclusion and Mission: The firm needs to put procedures in place that will reduce review time while maintaining or improving quality, even if it means increasing preparation time for some team members.

Introduction

Reviewing tax returns is a key part of tax preparation. It also is an area vulnerable to major bottlenecks and backlogs. Inevitably, firms have more preparers than reviewers. The latter are highly skilled professionals who are more difficult to train or find. Therefore, you must consider ways to reduce review time, even at the expense of adding preparer time.

This book will discuss methods to reduce review time, establish who should do the review, distinguish between content and issues review, identify specific items for the reviewer to check, and offer administrative procedures to facilitate the review process.

Reviewers are not born complete and ready to go, they are developed. The problem that I see with many firms is that they take a reasonably good tax return preparer, with above average tax knowledge and they make them a reviewer, either on purpose or by default. In many firms a partner doubles as a reviewer. In some cases this partner does not even have what I would consider reasonable tax knowledge, but they do the job because it needs to get done. This is not acceptable and does not assure a good product.

Part of the problem is that there is no information or training specifically for reveiwers, until now.

Being highly involved in managing tax season programs (since 1980 I have presented tax season management programs to over 5,000 CPAs through many organizations nationwide).

Actually, until December 2010, I have never heard of a program dedicated to tax return reviewers when I created a webinar. In preparing I wanted to include a reviewer's checklist. While all my travels and experience in this area not only have I never seen one, but I reached out to many colleagues in other firms and no one had one. I decided to create one, with Peter Weitsen's assistance (as he did with most of the checklists I've posted), to include in the webinar. I posted a comment on the New Jersey Society of CPA's Open Forum that I had one and would send to anyone requesting it. The first day I had 200 requests and within three days there were over 500 requests and downloads. The webinar ended up being presented five times from the end of December through mid-March 2011 with most of the programs sold out. I've also had many attendees call me with comments and questions.

This shows that there is a need and hunger for information on how to more effectively review returns, and this book is the response. Read the book, reread sections, use it as a reference source and email or call me if you have any questions or want to discuss anything about your review process. Your comments will be appreciated. Good luck on making your review process more effective.

CHAPTER 1:

Nature of Tax Return Preparation

Tax season is a microcosm of everything done in an accounting practice. One of the primary concerns of a business is having the proper processes and quality control procedures. Many firms, however, do not have uniform tax return review procedures, and even when they do, they are not always adhered to. Choosing how to properly use the reviewers' time and interface them with the staff can contribute immensely to a smooth tax season.

Because of the compression of work in a relatively short period, tax season provides an excellent opportunity for a continuous quality control initiative, the goal of which is reducing errors. Reviewers play a key role in reducing errors and setting and improving firm standards since they get to see the work of a large number of staff in a very short time period. This gives the reviewers insights into the work habits, pride, passion, quality, responsibility and ownership of these staff. The large volume going through the firm, and reaching the reviewers provides a unique opportunity to affect the overall quality of all the work done by these staff and not just the work on tax returns. If approached properly, tax return preparation can be the spearhead toward improving and elevating the quality of work done by everyone in the firm in every area they practice in.

Reviewers should be made aware of their role in these efforts. However, because of the huge volume and never ceasing deadlines, big picture quality methods are usually shunted aside in favor of getting the returns out. Firm management must become leaders in the quality effort and for that reason, they need to focus on the long-term benefits of processes that will elevate the level of work and enlist the reviewers into those initiatives.

Throughout this book are systems and procedures that are designed to raise the quality level of the firm as a whole. Coinciding with this are review methods and actions that will also, in the long run, reduce the time pressures of the reviewers, and also partners.

Tax return preparation work, if approached properly, will create lasting firm wide improvements. Use this as an opportunity for growth. Train the reviewers and empower them to go for it!

CHAPTER 2:

Review Procedures = Quality Control

The purpose of tax return reviews is to assure the quality of the return.

Quality should be defined as an accurate product along with pertinent and applicable tax law benefits applied as well as planning opportunities identified so the client could maximize their financial wealth and security.

Throughout this book I refer to the review process just as that – the review process. However, in reality it is part of the Quality Control ("QC") system. If you think of the review as QC would you look at tax return reviews differently?

Ask yourself if there is a difference between review and quality control? I think not! From my speaking to thousands of accountants across the country, it is my understanding that average review time is about 40% of the time it takes the preparer to do the return (not considering calls to get additional information and error correcting time). Consider your clients that have QC departments. How much time do you think they spend on average for QC? Would 5% seem right?

Accounting firms that have high review times usually have high error rates necessitating the higher review time. Doesn't that sound crazy? Why not set up procedures to reduce the error rate? I have been told that error rates range between 5% and 95%. 95%!!!??? That is crazy! There must be a time that you decide to reduce this amount.

You can rationalize all the expediency reasons in the world, but this is just bad... stupid... and poor business!

Six Important Questions To Ask Yourself

1. **Should QC need to be made a top priority for the firm, and especially the tax preparation process?**

   The higher QC time is, the greater your costs to prepare the return, the higher the error rate by the preparers, the longer it will take the return to go through the process, the higher your WIP inventory, the longer it will take to get paid and the more unhappy your staff and the client will be. Further, the greater the number of touches the more likelihood there is of an error.

2. **In your opinion, who should be responsible for QC?**

   a. The reviewer

   b. The partner

   c. The preparer

   d. The person assembling the return

   e. The client

   f. The IRS or tax agency

g. The managing partner. If he or she isn't responsible for QC, then they have a nice title, but they are not a leader.

If the managing partner is unable to deal with this, they can still be a leader by designating a champion for QC, develop with them a QC method and process, communicating it to the entire staff, empowering them, and then standing aside. Standing aside means not interfering with the process. It will be difficult... very difficult... the first tax season it is done, but it will be one of your smartest investments.

The problem with implementation is the complaints you will get from everyone else in the firm about the onerous procedures, and the temptation to calm them down by relaxing the standard or procedures the QC champion established. Giving in to that temptation will destroy the system while it is still in its infancy.

The biggest problem in execution is getting buy-in from, or a noninterference treaty with, your other partners and senior staff. The importance of this process has to be impressed upon them, and they must be made to understand that this decision has been made to make them richer and their work better, in the long run. They must be "hands-off."

If you think you are a leader, then this will be your first test!

Your main job after the plan is established would be to monitor compliance and back up the QC champion.

Believe me I know what I am talking about. If you have any questions, or want to discuss setting up an effective QC program, call me. I will be glad to talk with you.

3. If you don't think you need an effective QC program, consider:

    a. How many returns have errors that the person signing the return finds?

    b. How many errors does the assembler find?

    c. How many errors does the client find?

    d. How many errors does the tax agency find?

These questions deal solely with errors after the reviewer signs off on the return. Now find out how many errors the reviewer finds and has corrected. That would be much more than the above number of returns with errors.

Also, another issue is to find out how the returns with the errors got through the reviewer. The reviewer missed things they shouldn't have either because they didn't know something they should have, they weren't fully qualified, or they had reviewer fatigue because of being worn down by the never ending volume of error-filled returns they were forced to review. *Fix it!*

4. Do preparers check their work?

☐"Yes" or

☐"No"

What is your number of preparers' returns that have errors the reviewer finds?

☐ 5%,

☐ 25%,

☐ 50%,

☐ 75%,

☐ 95%

a. How do your preparers check their work?

    i.   Do they fill out the preparer's checklist?

    ii.   Do they clear all the diagnostic questions?

    iii.   Do they look at the completed return before handing in for review?

    iv.   Do they compare the completed return to last year's return?

    v.   Do they compare the completed return to the tax projection for that client?

    vi.   Do they fill out an "Ed Mendlowitz Excel Comparison Sheet?" *[See Appendix on Excel® tax comparison worksheets]*

    vii.   Do they separately calculate the tax?

    viii.   Do they look at size of refund or balance due to see if it looks "reasonable"?

    ix.   What do YOU do when you prepare a return to check yourself?

See the later section about the quality of a self-review. The reasons for doing so should be obvious—it will reduce overall time, conserve the reviewers' time, and create a more efficient process.

Actually, each of the above needs to be done. You need procedures to make sure these steps are implemented and followed.

5. When the partner gets the return to sign and they find an error, whose error is it?

a. the preparer's? Or

b. the reviewer's?

In my opinion it is the reviewer's error. The reviewer's job is to find the errors before passing on the return. Why did the reviewer make the error? See answer to Question 3 above for some reasons.

6. Are the checklists filled out deliberately, carefully and correctly?

a. By ☐ Preparer,

b. By ☐ Reviewer,

c. By ☐ anyone else,

d. By ☐ anyone?

The checklists should be filled out as the return is being worked on. Anything else would ruin your system. Some people treat the checklist as punishment for completing the work and check the boxes off just before they hand in the work.

CHAPTER 3:

Why Checklists
Are Critical

This is an area I feel very strongly about, and it is a major reason for the success of the better firms and the lack of growth of smaller firms.

By my way of thinking, a system must be established to assure the greatest quality at every level, reduce the number of touches per return, and present the client with the type of return he or she is relying on you to deliver. This system only works if there is strict adherence to the processes and procedures, and this includes the careful and deliberate use of checklists.

Here are a few main bullet points that explain what I believe and what I want to convey to you.

Nine Truths About Tax Season Management

1. Delegating means leveraging work, which creates opportunities for the delegator and delegatee

2. Opportunities for the delegator and delegatee mean professional growth in a planned, organized order

3. Delegating means trusting that what is needed to be done will be done the way it needs to be done

4. Firm systems create a method of training, supervision, oversight, and confidence that the work will be done the way it needs to be done

5. The system makes it easier to delegate and manage because a structure is in place

6. Checklists are part of the system and make it easier to lay out what needs to be done and how it should be done and in what order, and reduces instructions and doesn't cause relearning the system each time a job needs to be done

7. Not doing the checklists the right way cancels everything I just said and creates added work and the need for more supervisio

8. Not doing the checklists also reduces profits; remember that you are running a business

9. Not doing checklists increases stress and reduces the enjoyment in what you do

Most people do not like filling out checklists. Why? I don't know because I like them.

"Checklists create order, cause me to not reinvent the wheel every time I need to do something I previously did, create a place where I can list things that need to be done that won't be forgotten, help me make sure I cover everything I am supposed to cover, and enable me to more easily pass on what I know and have learned from my experiences." Now you read the last sentence out loud as if you wrote it and read it as if you mean it and if your procedures are different, but you believe this is the way it should be, then MAKE IT HAPPEN!

Checklists also make it easier to assure the quality of work and procedures of people you supervise. Despite these many benefits, many staff members do not like to fill them out, including both less- and more-experienced staff and even some partners.

The issue with many checklists – and this is especially so with income tax preparation – is that the checklists are just too long. The AICPA Tax Section checklists and PPC Tax Preparation checklists run over 20 pages; however, in these instances there is a very good reason for their length. Tax returns are very complicated, requiring a myriad range of knowledge that most preparers, many reviewers, and few partners possess. The problem with such long checklists is that they take too long to follow making it cost prohibitive for most tax returns. Because of this, they are not used, and then neither are any other checklists.

Where they are supposed to be used, many firms look the other way, knowing the completed checklists were not read. In my opinion, these acts destroy your quality control system.

Tax returns take time. At many firms, the newer staff (read: less experienced) prepare returns. In some firms, very experienced audit staff take time off from their audits to prepare or, worse, review returns. That quality must be assured is a given, yet procedures are followed that cause reduced quality, a poor result, greater overall time spent on the returns, greater time spent by the overstressed reviewers, and less profits.

If it were up to me, I would have a zero tolerance policy for noncompliance with checklists and procedures, no matter how busy things get.

If you are not using checklists, you must start ASAP! Adapt some of the checklists I prepared. If you want a Word file email me and I'll email you every checklist referred to in this book. No charge! My pleasure!

CHAPTER 4:

Content Review Versus Issue Review

Each type of review requires a different discipline. The two primary types of reviews are content and issues. In content review the preparer checks most or all of the original client info and determines whether it has been entered and used correctly. This review is very time consuming, and although a lower level staff person can do it, a tax department specialist usually does. We find that this type of review does not add value. It might improve the accuracy of the return, but it doesn't make the client richer. This is sometimes called a "tick and tie" review.

An issues review purely adds value. Not only are tax issues examined to see if applicable, but the focus is also on planning for the current year and finding ways to make the client richer.

In an ideal world, everything that should be done would be done with the proper time allowed for each step. Also, preparers and reviewers must understand that the tax return must be properly prepared – with the input carefully and correctly entered; with an understanding of what information might be missing; with tax savings, planning, compliance issues deliberately considered; and with "outside the box" planning considered such as financial, retirement, or family security issues developed or brought to the clients' attention as the return is being prepared and reviewed by the accounting firm.

Now, back to reality. Any human endeavor has errors. The issue becomes one of where you want the errors to occur – in missing a charity receipt, or overlooking an opportunity to provide advice on opening a SEP, contributing to a Roth IRA, enrolling in his or her employer's 401k plan, or choosing types of mutual funds. Looking at the big picture instead of every small detail helps to save time and catch mistakes, while not sacrificing quality.

By the way, the proper handling of errors found by the client or a government agency can be an opportunity for the firm. If the error is quickly identified, acknowledged, and rectified, the client often will gain a greater confidence in the firm than if the error hadn't been made. However, I do not recommend this as a method of client bonding.

CHAPTER 5:

Effectiveness and Purpose of Review

Following is a summary of review procedures often followed in the busiest time of tax season versus the way it should be followed.

April 1-15 has been selected to refer to the final and busiest period of tax season.

If yours starts earlier or ends earlier, substitute those dates for what I chose.

Some steps have been abbreviated.

April 1-15

What Often Happens	What Should Happen
Reviewers cannot teach	Reviewers are teachers
Reviewers cut corners	Reviewers are guardians of the procedures and follow them diligently
Reviewers skip looking at last year's return (but look at Excel® tax comparison worksheets if firm uses them)	Reviewers compare to last year's return for names, addresses, dependents and Social Security numbers, and categories and amounts on return (or looks at Excel® tax comparison worksheets if firm uses them)
Reviewers bypass checklists and relax requirement of making preparer complete checklists	Reviewers look at checklists and explain deficiencies to preparers, and insist checklists be followed completely
Reviewers make changes instead of staff who are not available	Reviewers make lists of errors and explain to preparers what they did wrong and have preparers make the changes. Alternatively reviewers can call in the preparer and explain each error and what needs to be done to correct it and not have error reoccur
Reviewers primarily look for big differences and look at big numbers	Reviewers primarily look for big differences and look at big numbers
Reviewers look for big issues and skip looking at all the detail	Reviewers look for big issues and skip looking at all the detail

Not every one of the abbreviated April 1-15 procedures is bad. Compare the last two procedures to what goes on the rest of year for many firms. Are you one of them?

April 1-15 (recommended for all year)	Rest of year (what many firms do and I don't recommend at all)
Reviewers primarily look for big differences and look at big numbers	Reviewers look at every number (they spend their time ticking and tying)
Reviewers look for big issues and skip looking at all the detail	Reviewers don't really look for big issues – time is consumed ticking and tying and looking at all the detail

First ask yourself what your procedures are and if they are different during your busiest period.

Next ask yourself, if you change your procedures during your busiest period, why don't you just adopt those procedures all year round?

Obviously, I do not like the April 1-15 column for the items except for the last two items which are the only two items that are the same on the rest of year column.

To be clear, my recommended procedures for all year round are:

Year Round Review Procedures

Reviewers are teachers

Reviewers are guardians of the procedures and follow them diligently

Reviewers compare to last year's return for names, addresses, dependents and Social Security numbers and categories and amounts on return (or looks at Excel® tax comparison worksheets if firm uses them)

Reviewers look at checklists and explain deficiencies to preparers, and insist checklists be followed completely

Reviewers make lists of errors and explain to preparers what they did wrong and have preparers make the changes. Alternatively reviewers can call in the preparer and explain each error and what needs to be done to correct it and not have error reoccur

Reviewers primarily look for big differences and look at big numbers

Reviewers look for big issues and skip looking at all the detail

I am not imposing the Excel® tax comparison worksheets, but very highly recommend using them for all except the simplest of returns. (see Appendix)

Tax season review procedures need to be self-assessed. The big issue I see is that the rush causes some desirable "short-cuts" such as the last two items and many undesirable short-cuts which get the return out sooner but has a cost of breaking down the system and having you have to start over each year with the same problems of untrained or poorly trained people not following procedures and making the same type of mistakes they always made. Shouldn't this stop?

Imagine everyone cooking a Big Mac® in McDonald's sidestepping the procedures so the hamburgers could get made faster and the customers getting served quicker? That is what you are doing, except instead of Big Macs® it is your clients' tax returns that your staff will NEVER get right (unless by extreme accident)!

Three Questions For You To Consider When You Decide On A Method Of Reviewing Returns

1. Evaluate the results and consequences when the ticking and tying is not done. Is the error rate on those returns greater or less than the error rate on returns prepared the rest of year with the ticking and tying as measured by:

    a. Partners catch more or fewer errors when they sign those returns

    b. Clients catch more or fewer errors when they look over those returns

    c. More (or the same or fewer) notices sent by tax agencies on those returns

2. Are more or fewer bigger issues found by reviewers and partners during the period of not ticking and tying:

    a. Recommending SEPs

    b. Finding rollovers not reflected properly

c. Current year planning issues raised

d. Other big issues

3. How does your staff perform during April 1 – 15:

   a. Do they spend less time per return?

   b. Do they get responses to requests for missing information faster?

   c. Do they have fewer touches?

   d. Do they have greater recollection of issues when they pick up return to add missing info and complete; or to fix errors?

I believe most of your answers will indicate there is not any loss of quality or efficiency. There might even be an increase! Based on your answers to the above questions, why not follow the April 1 - 15 procedures during the entire year?

If you disagree and get really bad returns prepared, then you won't want to short-cut your procedures. However, this means that the quality of what is turned in for review by your staff is terrible.

You drive the train, not the other way around. It is the process that governs, not the people that are unhappy having to follow the procedures.

Methods To Reduce Review Time

To have a successful tax season, care and effort must be spent to reduce the review time while maintaining quality. The reviewer's time is the main element that needs to be managed and reduced.

Some ways this can be accomplished follow:

Seven Best Practices

1. Better training of the preparers.

2. Better training of the reviewers.

3. Digitization as much as possible, such as reviewing the returns on screen and reducing printing and paper handling; reviewing the backup on an indexed digital file; electronically transferring K-1s when the corporate, partnership, or trust returns are prepared by the firm; carrying forward carryover and pro forma data kept track of by the tax preparation software; filling out client organizers online and transferring them into the current year's program.

4. Modularization or compartmentalization of the work so it can be

done and reviewed more easily.

5. Better scheduling of the work so the more complicated returns are not bunched together and can be reviewed calmly and separately.

6. Creating a less harried, less hurried office atmosphere.

Keeping everything in order and in its place. For example, make sure accountants clean their desks every night.

CHAPTER 6:

Reviewer's Checklists

Following are two reviewer's checklists – for individual and business returns. I've tried to keep these as short as possible. The reviewer can always use preparer's checklists that are more thorough and complete.

One way for the reviewer checklist to be used is for the reviewer to give it to the preparer and tell the preparer to make sure that the reviewer will be able to easily find the information they need to in order to perform their review easily.

For firms that insist on having all the detail ticked and tied, a suggestion is to have another preparer pre-review the detail input. Having a person at the same level as the preparer review the input will push the work down from the reviewer; serve to help the same level reviewer hone their skills at locating the types and frequency of errors; and might create peer pressure to not have someone at the same level find their errors.

Reviewer's Checklist For Individual Tax Returns

Client_____ Year_____ Date _____

Prepared_____ By_____

Following is a suggested checklist of things for the reviewer to do:

☐ Review client's name and address, Social Security numbers and business code (if applicable) if this is first year doing this client's return

☐ Review Excel tax comparison worksheet – current and prior year's summary information, and projection if one was prepared, and explanations for large variances, differences, inconsistent amounts, and surprise items

☐ Compare last year's return with this year's return if Excel worksheet was not prepared

☐ Were last year's unusual or large items reviewed to see if they were applicable for this year

☐ Verify that estimated tax payments were made

☐ Review that estimated tax payments were entered properly on Tax Payments Worksheet

☐ Review that estimated payments were calculated properly for the current year

☐ Review K-1 input

☐ Review W-2 input

☐ Total of all 1099 income should tie in with amounts on return

☐ Were carryforwards entered properly and accounted for

☐ Were suspended losses properly treated

☐ Were gross sales from security transactions reconciled with 1099s (use form we have for this)

☐ Review cost basis on 1099s and return for wash sales, gifted and inherited stocks

☐ Compare federal to state returns to see that add backs and reductions seem logical

☐ If a trial balance or financial statement was provided for client's Schedule C business, reconcile any book to tax differences or adjustments, and that they appear reasonable

☐ Make sure items on flag sheets, notes based on discussions with client during the year, special instructions and knowledge points in tax control were considered

☐ Look at client's correspondence and notes that accompanied tax information to see if applicable to the tax return preparation or if it requires separate follow up actions

☐ Address any notes or comments by a partner

☐ Look at tax notices for last year to see if they affect current year's
return

☐ Should be no diagnostics, open or unresolved items

☐ Were all questions on the preparer's checklist answered. Should
be no unanswered items

☐ Address S Corporation distributions to client in excess of AAA or
with negative capital

☐ If self-employment income, was a SEP or other pension plan
payment made or considered

☐ If client did not make maximum IRA contributions, were they
made aware of it

☐ Was question for foreign bank accounts or signatory powers checked and Form TDF 90-22.1 prepared if required

☐ If not checked, was client asked if they had a foreign account or signatory powers:

___Yes, ___No

(If no, make sure they are asked question)

☐ Review AMT adjustments, calculations and opportunities to use AMT credit from prior years

☐ Are filing and estimated tax instructions correct

☐ All penalties, interest, underpayment and late filing penalties should be calculate

☐ Look at every page of completed return and review for any obvious red flags or audit triggers

☐ Was there any follow through by client on tax or financial planning recommendations made last year Report any comments:

_____

_____

_____

☐ Were opportunities identified for tax or financial planning for the client. This should be followed up after tax season. Put on tax calendar with date. If not included on separate checklist, list here:

_____

_____

Reviewer's Checklist For Business Tax Returns

Client_____ **Year**____ **Date** _____

Prepared_____ **By**_____

☐ Did audit manager of this client review the input and result

Yes____ No____

☐ Review client's name and address, business code, State of incorporation and all EINs and owners ([1]) Social Security numbers if this is first year doing this client's return

☐ Pass through entities: managing owner should have submitted an updated address list

_____

[1] The term owners will be used to refer to stockholders, partners or members, as the case may be

☐ Pass through entities with change in ownership: verify that the dates of change and income allocations were entered and allocated properly

☐ For first year, make sure all the proper elections have been made such as accounting basis, inventory method, Section 263A, S elections (including State), mark to market for traders, depreciation and amortization. For later years make sure return is consistent with elections

☐ Make sure all questions on return have been answered

☐ Determine that accounting basis listed on the tax return is consistent with the income statement and balance sheet presentation on tax return (for example, if the cash basis is checked, make sure the balance sheet on the tax return is prepared using the cash basis; and that there are no A/R, bad debts, A/P or inventory for a cash basis company)

☐ Tie in retained earnings or capital accounts balances with trial balance (^{2}) and tax return

☐ Make sure the time spent by officers is reflected as a percentage and not as "all" or "part"

☐ Review book to tax adjustment reconciliation and tie in totals to trial balance

☐ If financial statement was prepared, look at note regarding income taxes for inconsistencies

☐ Determine that the individual amounts on book to tax reconciliation appear reasonable

☐ Check that cash balance on tax return agrees with year-end bank reconciliations

_____

[2] Even though "trial balance" may be used in this checklist, you can use the Company's financial statements if that was what was used for the preparation of the tax return, or computer generated statements

- ☐ Check that totals of fixed assets and accumulated depreciation and amortization on balance sheet of tax return agrees with depreciation and amortization schedules

- ☐ Verify that gross payroll on tax return agrees with gross payroll on W-3

- ☐ Tie in total of all 1099s company prepared with amounts on return

- ☐ Reconcile sales on the client's sales tax returns with the sales on the income tax return

- ☐ If company is on accrual basis, were accruals timely paid after year end

- ☐ Determine if pension accruals were properly calculated, timely, properly paid, and correctly shown on balance sheet

- ☐ Was interest properly paid, received, or accrued on loans to/from related parties

☐ Obtain explanations for large variances, differences, inconsistent amounts, and surprise items appearing on tax return as compared to prior year and/or projections if prepared

☐ Were estimated tax payments entered properly on Tax Payments Worksheet

☐ Were estimated payments calculated properly for the current year (If a C Corp and earnings over $1 million any one of last three years, different estimated tax payment rules apply)

☐ Are there unreasonable compensation or unreasonable accumulation of earnings issues

☐ Review K-1 input and tie in to distributions and investments during the year per the books

☐ Were carryforwards entered properly and accounted for

☐ Were gross sales from security transactions reconciled with 1099s (use form we have for this)

☐ Compare federal to state returns to see that add backs and reductions seem logical

☐ Address S Corporations that had distributions in excess of AAA or with negative capital

☐ Were there foreign relationships, transactions or ownership which require special forms such as 8804, 5471, 5472 or TDF 90-22.1

☐ Were items on flag sheets, notes based on discussions with client during the year, special instructions and knowledge points in tax control considered

☐ Look at client's correspondence and notes that accompanied tax information to see if applicable to the tax return preparation or if it requires separate follow up actions

☐ Address any notes or comments by a partner

☐ Look at tax notices for last year to see if they affect current year's return

☐ Should be no diagnostics, open or unresolved items

☐ Were all questions on the preparer's checklist answered. Should be no unanswered items

☐ Are filing and estimated tax instructions correct

☐ All penalties, interest, underpayment and late filing penalties should be calculated

☐ Look at every page of completed return and review for any obvious red flags or audit triggers

☐ Was there any follow through by client on tax or planning recommendations made last year. Report any comments:

_____

_____

_____

☐ Were opportunities identified for tax or planning for the client. This should be followed up after tax season. Put on tax calendar with date. List here:

_____

_____

_____

Top 12 Tax Return Preparation Errors

1. Number transposition and spelling errors.

This includes income and deduction amounts and client Social Security numbers, addresses and zip codes. Spelling errors should also be avoided – they indicate a lack of attention to what you are doing.

2. Unreported 1099 income.

Clients frequently leave out 1099s, but the preparer should make sure all 1099 items from last year are accounted for. Missing 1099s that were not final for last year should be accounted for.

3. Tax payments.

Entering incorrect and unpaid amounts can be avoided by requiring the client to provide "proof" of the payments. Entering "incorrect" amounts provided by the client is a major cause of tax notices.

4. Keeping review notes after the return is completed.

This can create liability issues if there is ever a controversy over the return. Review notes usually deal with errors and omissions and the type and quantity of them can indicate a lack of training, proper procedures, adherence to processes or care. Retaining these notes can never help you.

5. Not correcting reason for tax notices for prior year on this year's return.

This is a no brainer, but for many preparers there is a disconnect between a notice for last year's return and the preparing of this year's return.

6. Not questioning numbers that stretch the imagination.

My imagination is likely to be different from yours, but a client with high debt indicated by mortgage and home equity loan interest usually won't be making cash charitable contributions equal to 8 percent of their gross income. Likewise for maximum allowable IRA contributions. Explain the requirements for substantiating these deductions and ask client if they have it.

7. **Not following up enough with clients to get missing information.**

   This could create last minute rushes and unhappy clients, even though it was because of client's lack of response.

8. **Not specifically asking clients if they have, can sign or control a foreign bank account.**

9. **Not telling client about items that aren't on return.**

   Items such as traditional and Roth IRAs, SEPs, making charitable contributions with appreciated stock, claiming a grown child with minimal income who lives with client as a dependent, or signing up for an employer's 401k plan and/or flexible spending account, or partial exercising of ISOs to avoid AMT.

10. **High mortgage interest deductions.**

    Excessive amounts (usually over $50,000) are a red flag for the IRS. Make sure the interest is not from excessive mortgages, that the funds were used for proper purposes or that the interest tracking rules have been complied with and if mortgage proceeds were used for investment purposes, it is properly reflected on the return.

11. Alternative minimum tax.

Watch for unapplied AMT credits and AMT NOLs, and state tax refunds reported as income even though not deducted in prior year because of AMT.

12. Not calling a client to relay unexpected (or especially bad) final results.

Any errors uncovered by the checklists need to be corrected by the preparer. It is important to remember part of the training process is for the preparer, not the reviewer, to make any necessary changes, even though it might be a simple change.

CHAPTER 7:

Good Preparer Procedures Will Reduce Review Time

The better the quality of the return submitted to the reviewer, the easier it will be for the reviewer and they could spend more time using their brain instead of their eyes.

Here is a procedural checklist for preparers to follow. Probably a better way would be for the preparer to use the reviewer's checklist.

Preparer's Pre-Review Procedural Checklist

☐ Compare the completed return to last year's return and make sure there are no great differences.

☐ Use the tax comparison feature to compare the last year's categories to this year's or prepare and review Excel® tax comparison worksheet.

☐ Look at the completed return that you just did to see that it makes sense and that there are no glaring errors.

☐ Use uniform procedures and worksheets wherever possible.

☐ Make sure that all worksheets, schedules and lead sheets tie into amounts on the tax return.

☐ Respond to all open items in the software diagnostics so there are no items left for the reviewer to resolve or follow up on.

☐ Complete all checklists after reading them.

☐ Indicate whether another preparer pre-reviewed the detail input and enter their name here: _____ .

☐ Make sure you responded to all items you could if reviewer asked you to follow the *Reviewer's Checklist.*

Many procedures whose purpose is to reduce reviewer's time will add to the preparer's time and occasionally will add to the total time for the return. That is so and acceptable since there are more preparers and they are usually at lower levels than the reviewer, and it is with the reviewers where bottlenecks develop. Further the cost and billing rates for reviewers is substantially greater than for preparers so savings of reviewer time can actually reduce the time charges for the returns where there is the tradeoff.

Added effort by the preparer will save reviewers' time. We have found that requiring extensive, complete, neat, organized, and indexed working papers or PDF files will take about 20 minutes extra a return to do, but will reduce the time it takes the preparer to prepare a return by about an hour and 20 minutes – net gain one hour per return. (Note: I am not talking about simple tax returns, but those of some complexity.)

For a workload of 400 returns, this reduces the time by the equivalent of one full-time person during tax season. Smartscanners are now performing many of these functions.

CHAPTER 8:

Effective Self-Reviews Improve Efficiency

It occurs to me that there is a difference in the quality between the returns someone does for themself and the returns they do for their clients.

An informal survey by me showed that the percentage of returns with errors of sole practitioners and partners in CPA firms is less than 2%, while the percentage of errors by their staff ranges from a low of 30% to a high of 95%! Why the difference?

It seems that there are two primary reasons –

1. knowing that someone will check everything; and
2. knowing that no one will check the work.

I don't believe work is done as carefully if it is known that someone will be rechecking everything that was done. There are three ways to use this knowledge to have better returns prepared by staff and use the reviewers more effectively.

1. One way to solve this problem is to not recheck everything – usually referred to as "ticking and tying" – but to let it be known that there will only be spot checks or brief, but selective, overviews; and that errors are the full responsibility of the preparer.

2. Another way is to have the preparer tie in everything and close off the work papers assuming everything is perfect and will need no changes.

This will cause a big annoyance and much more work if errors are found. However, by using this method I have seen that the quality of the preparers' work is greatly improved with much less time being spent by reviewers and much lower overall time spent on the return, albeit the extra inconvenience and cost of reopening the closed files.

The objective is a better return with quicker turnaround and higher quality, and that is usually the result. The higher quality comes from the reviewers being better able to look for issues and planning opportunities rather than errors in arithmetic on grouping sheets and missed charity deductions.

Note that this method is for returns done by people competent to do the work, and not people you are training or teaching; however, this method can be adapted to any level of preparer.

This only works if followed completely and the firm leader has the resolve to insist on this and the strength to ignore the whining and complaints about the "extra" work (by the people who make the errors).

I strictly followed this procedure and it did not win me any popularity awards, but the quality of the returns submitted by the preparer was greatly elevated, making tax season much calmer and everyone happier. (But I still wasn't given any award!) You have to decide what you are trying to accomplish.

3. A third way is to delegate the "ticking and tying" (if you feel a compulsion to have it done) to a peer preparer, before it is turned in to the reviewer

I have used all three of these methods and they all result in a better product, less cost, and quicker turnaround than a method where the reviewer rechecks everything. Another method which I have recently begun advocating is to change the name of the "review department" to "quality control department." I believe this will decrease the error rate because of QC's stronger identity with quality. Also, everyone knows that the QC people rarely recheck everything.

Knowing that no one will check the tax return causes a much more deliberate and thorough self-review. Proof of this is the small amount of errors made by people preparing their own tax returns. "Errors on a return" is defined by either a tax agency notice being sent to correct or call attention to an error, finding an error yourself after the return has been filed, such as when you are preparing a subsequent year's return, or the client calling you to say they found an error. In the office for clients' returns you can also define an error as one that is caught by the partner as she was about to sign off on the return.

Assuming I am correct, then if a system could be initiated to have the preparers in a firm do a better job of reviewing their own work before handing it in, then overall quality will be improved and once again you will be reducing the most dear time during tax season – that of the reviewers – oops, that of the QC people.

None of the above involves additional teaching or training in taxes, but it does require a major change in the firm's and preparer's mindset. If I might suggest, it requires a change of culture to one of extremely low tolerance for errors. This change generally starts at the top and works its way down, so the partners need to buy-in to it before you start, and remain in during tax season.

In some instances, I have seen highly improved QC with isolated reviewers working on their own who take the time to insist preparers give them good work. They set the standard and teach it one on one to those who will be passing work to them. Usually this change starts with consternation but results in better work all around, happier staff, and a highly quality return for the client. And greater profits!

My challenge to you is to consider your internal procedures and decide if you are satisfied with them. If so, then good for you! However, if you believe a change is in order, why not consider what I said above and try it?

I also refer you back to the table comparing the reviews done April 1 – 15 versus the rest of the year. Another informal survey by me indicates that there is no increase in the amount of notices sent on a percentage basis by tax agencies for returns done during April 1 – 15; there is also better turnaround and a higher quality return because of fewer preparer errors because the preparers understand that the review won't be as thorough so they do a better initial job.

Moat significantly, you'll get a more focused issue review, which is really the best way to use the reviewers' brains, experience, and training.

CHAPTER 9:

Reviewing Outsourced Returns

There are different types of outsourced returns. Returns prepared in India, Texas, smart scanner data-populated returns, other CPA firms, per diem people working at home and even your staff working at home.

Be aware that your review procedures should be the same regardless of how or where the returns are prepared.

One extra step that I would recommend when first using an outside service is to have a preparer check the input, and after confidence is achieved, then to spot check about a quarter to third of the input.

Many people outsource part or all of their return preparation to companies in India. Some of the India companies send crews to Texas or another place in the United States to avoid the offshore disclosure. Many are now using smart scanners that populate the tax software programs. All of the three services mentioned also deliver organized and indexed digital work papers. A number of firms – including some national firms and major public companies – prepare returns for CPA firms on an outsourced basis. Another source are per diem people working at home and even your own staff. Conceptually, everyone preparing tax returns works independent of the other people in the firm. Two people sitting at a joint table working on returns are working independently of the other. Reviewers receive most of their work digitally which include the completed returns and backup; they send comments digitally and receive the responses the same way. Everyone that does returns, on some level, is an outsource source. The only difference is how they are paid and where they physically sit.

Procedures to prepare and review returns must be systemized with the reviewers primarily responsible to make sure the preparers follow the system, complete the mandatory worksheets and have lead sheets that tie their work into the amounts entered on the return. Where the Excel tax comparison worksheet is used, that becomes the nerve center for the review, and also is the preparer's self-checking mechanism.

Outsourcing (which I have said includes every preparation method) presents a big opportunity to train preparers to review by having them review the input – at first completely and then on a spot check basis. Reviewing is an important discipline and this offers a look-see at preparers to determine who might have the qualities to become future reviewers.

For those that haven't tried it yet, smart scanners are a fabulous tool, which, if used correctly can save time and cost. The one thing they do not do is check their work. However, smart scanners do not need lunch or dinner brought into the office and don't take coffee or smoke breaks; but they do organize the digital work papers on your internal filing system and you don't have to listen to how their weekend day off was.

Eight Typical Errors To Watch Out For

1. Previous year information picked up on the current year return because of a wrong 1099 or W-2 that was sent

2. K-1s being picked up on wrong lines, or not enough information picked up. This is a typical error with smart scanners and needs to be reviewed carefully

3. Failure to pick up foreign tax credit amounts properly

4. Data was missing that was reported on the previous year return and accounts weren't closed

5. Carry-forward information not reflected properly

6. Name spelling, lists of dependents and Social Security numbers should always be checked

7. Boxes that were checked in prior year are not checked in current year such as presidential campaign fund and foreign bank accounts

8. Actually, the reviewers' checklist covers the most prevalent errors – have the preparer use that checklist before they submit the return for review

CHAPTER 10:

Review of Complicated Transactions

One way of reducing the busiest time bottlenecks is by having complicated issues reviewed when they arise, or before tax season gets hot and heavy. Many times it can save a lot of time by the preparer, or partner, having a discussion with the reviewer before transaction is completed to make sure it is structured correctly. I've done this many times and have also got a great second opinion that helped the transaction get done better.

19 Examples Of Complicated Transactions That Delay The Review Process

1. 1245 and 1250 recaptures

2. 1231 losses

3. 754 basis step up – these can be reviewed as soon as the estate or sale is signed off on

4. Payment of personally guaranteed debt of a dissolved S corporation or C corporation

5. Section 1244 losses

6. Purchase/sale price allocations and intangibles

7. Grantor trust flow through amounts, reporting of them and verification that the trust did not get and use its own TIN

8. Termination during the year of the grantor's right to affect transactions that make the trust no longer a grantor trust

9. Transfers during the year of partnership and S corporation ownership interests

10. Allocation of estimated tax payments for a couple that was divorced during the year

11. Get copies of divorce and separation agreements when executed to ascertain tax treatment

12. Employment severance payments

13. Deferred compensation agreements or payments

14. Employee exercising incentive stock options or non-qualified stock options or receiving and/or selling restricted stock

15. Sales of a business

16. Sales of rental property

17. Sales of vacation homes or non-primary residences

18. Donations of art work or other assets with a value greater than $5,000

19. Sale of very low basis property in an S corporation where the shareholder has a very high basis in their stock (such as when they purchased the stock of a C corporation and elected S status and the BIG period expired) to make sure the S corporation is liquidated in the year of sale so the basis can be applied

All of the above take place during the year and there is no reason why the transactions cannot be reviewed as they occur. Also, there is paperwork that usually accompanies the transactions and that needs to also be received and reviewed as soon as the closing.

CHAPTER 11:

Training and Assigning Reviewers

Firms have to decide who will do the review, and how are they qualified. Ideally, trained tax department personnel are the primary reviewers. However, the bunching and compression of work often shifts some of the review to higher level, non tax personnel such as audit managers and partners who might not have the comprehensive training, background, and experience to handle everything that comes up during the tax preparation process.

Additionally, in many firms, almost everyone on the staff will prepare some returns to ease the almost insurmountable burden on the tax department. That lack of trained preparers, though, places an added burden on the tax reviewers, making it important for them to have the range of experience needed to perform the review.

Reviewing returns is usually done by preparers with an above average knowledge of taxes who express interest in advancing in the tax specialty. They take added tax CPE, actually read the tax articles in the journals they subscribe to, think about unusual tax rulings and decisions, talk taxes with their buddies and associates at other firms, seek graduate degrees in taxes and develop an ability in article writing and speech presenting. I feel the staff person needs to express the interest and not be conscripted by their boss.

I know many non tax specialist managers and partners that feel they could review returns, but, in my opinion, they lack the broad range of knowledge and experience to do a reasonable job.

They spend their time ticking and tying and consider this as an adequate review, but it isn't since they do not have the ability to identify or uncover issues, or flush out opportunities for either the current return they are reviewing or planning for the next tax year.

I suggest giving any person that might be reviewing returns a short test to determine whether they have the basic knowledge a reviewer will need for situations they might encounter. These questions are suggestions and can be tailored to the type of practice you have and issues reviewers might come across.

Reviewers also need to be familiar with the processes and procedures and have patience and ability to train and insist that procedures be followed, and have a consistent record of adherence to the system. Shortcutters will never make good reviewers.

The 10-Question Reviewer Qualification Test

Whether or not you agree with all the questions below, you must consider a method for making sure reviewers are qualified. Doing so should also include reviewer-appropriate CPE and in-house training.

1. What is the latest date a simplified employee pension (SEP) plan can be opened for last year for a sole proprietor?

2. What date is used as the "date purchased" to report a stock transaction that includes an unallowed loss because there was a previous wash sale?

3. Are extra payments made to an ex-spouse to cover unanticipated increases in tuition in her nursing school deductible as alimony?

4. What is the maximum federal capital gains tax rate from any portion of the gain on commercial real estate that an individual tax client sells?

5. When would you use the annualization exception for the 2210 penalty?

6. How are individuals taxed on section 1256 gains?

7. How would you advise a client who makes large amounts of annual charitable contributions and typically reports large long-term capital gains?

8. What cost basis is used when a client sells immediately upon vesting employer-issued restricted stock shares that had no cost and the stockbroker has provided a 1099-B showing proceeds of $8,100? Use an approximate amount for the cost basis for your answer.

9. What would a minimum strategy be for a client with incentive stock options to avoid or partially avoid the alternative minimum tax (AMT)?

10. What is the equivalent taxable interest amount for a client with 4% municipal bond interest if his or her marginal federal tax rate is 25% (assume no state tax)?

See Appendix for Answers.

CHAPTER 12:

The MBWA Big Picture

Everyone gets caught up doing their own job during tax season. Preparers prepare and reviewers review. Partners meet with clients and get information, and sign returns before they are sent to client. Admin people do their thing as does the person scheduling the work. Who looks at the big picture?

Firms need someone to step back and look at the big picture. It's a function of leadership and management.

Someone has to be responsible for everyone doing their jobs and for firm systems to be followed. Usually it is a managing partner but can also be an HR or admin partner, or the partner heading the tax department. It cannot be a partner concerned with the numbers of his chargeable hours since big picture management is a MBWA [Managing By Wandering Around] job.

Firms with the MBWA person seem to work better, have less stress and pressure, more fun and more effective and efficient work flow. Someone has to step up and it is usually a person with less of a compliance work load than the others and who also feels the weight of responsibility that the firm functions smoothly with clients work getting done in the best way possible.

With respect to the reviewers, the MBWA partner will monitor their workload and potential for bottleneck and will head that off before it becomes critical. The MBWAer will also look at the reviewer and make sure he or she doesn't get caught up or bogged down on one sticky item. It will also give the reviewer someone to speak to about the work flow and overall quality in an informal way. This is unrecognized but important support for the reviewer.

I can tell from experience the frustration that sets in with a reviewer when the quality is not good. This is especially upsetting when higher level staff people prepare error-riddled returns. The MBWAer shares that frustration and takes some of the burden of the poor quality away because of the authority the MBWAer has.

CHAPTER 13:

Accountability

Reviewers have to face accountability. They are judged several ways, but I feel the best way is not with a metric but by how the quality of the preparers improve during tax season and how the workload is managed.

Yes, the reviewers are responsible for the preparers' quality. The reviewers are expected to find errors and show the preparer what they are, how to fix it and to not have them reoccur. And this should be done quickly – not letting prepared returns hang around unchecked for a while. The quicker the turnaround time, the easier and better the training and better all around job by everyone.

One of my key elements is for the preparer to make EVERY correction – even the easy changes that a reviewer can make in a "second." The preparers will learn by their mistakes, realize that their mistakes will have a bothersome cost to themselves by having to make arrangements to fix them, and I believe will reinforce the importance of quality with the first touch – not the second or third time around.

The reviewers will have a mounting workload since there are more preparers than reviewers. Workload management is an important part of the reviewers' job. When the workload becomes unmanageable the reviewer should seek assistance from the partner on prioritizing the review work and also added help. If the procedures are sound with the preparer doing the right type of job, the reviewer's work should be easier and will have less ticking and tying and more issues oriented consideration. This is the time when training and good systems really pay off. However, the time to get these in place is before tax season begins, not in the heat of the moment, although it is never too late to institute sound procedures.

We are accountants and measuring things is important and should be comfortable for us.

Here are some metrics that can be assessed after tax season to evaluate the overall performance of the preparers and reviewers...

Post Tax Season Performance Metrics

Reviewer's name_____	Total for reviewer	Specific preparer	Specific preparer	Specific preparer
# returns reviewed				
# returns with errors				
# returns with errors a 2nd time				
# returns with errors a 3rd time				
# returns that were approved by reviewer that had errors discovered by partner or client or someone else				
Time spent reviewing returns of each preparer				
Average review time per return				
Percent of review time based on total time sent by preparers				

# issues uncovered or recommended	This could be the most important		

How can you measure this?

This, to me, is the most important job of the reviewer, but it is not a metric you can easily develop. Many firms that bother to measure anything at all measure to their comfort level of what they can get results for.

This is the WRONG WAY to approach it. I also know firms that measure everything, but evaluate nothing!

Eight More Ways To Evaluate Staff And Tax Season

1. Staff that make repeated errors

2. Staff that don't listen to instructions

3. Staff that don't follow procedures or omit required standardized workpapers or lead sheets

4. Staff that continuously miss deadlines

5. Staff that always seem to work under pressure

6. Staff that clients complain about who don't return calls or are unresponsive to their questions

7. Staff that can't seem to finish anything

8. Staff who do not keep the partner or manager informed of their progress and questions and concerns of clients

I believe it is the responsibility of the reviewer to note these things and discuss with a partner. Quality is paramount and must be given a super high priority. I really think a zero tolerance attitude toward mistakes needs to be instituted. (I know – I keep repeating this!)

Reviewers need to look at quality from a very selfish standpoint. The better the quality in the work assigned to them, the less work they will do, the lower the backlog, the lower the tedium for them, the more issues they will develop and the more enjoyment and satisfaction they will get from their jobs.

CHAPTER 14:

Administrative Procedures

Reviewers are the team leaders of tax season. There are many people involved in the process, but an aware reviewer can and should be the team leader.

Every return passes through the review department. Some reviewers, like some staff and even some partners, do what they are supposed to do and they do it well and with pride, but they do not step over the boundary of what they perceive their job is to do. The leaders step forward and assume responsibility!

Many reviewers get stuck in a slot and remain there. Nothing wrong with that and maybe the use of the word stuck is not appropriate. Maybe I should have said placed. Many reviewers get placed in a slot and remain there. Sounds better. Now, nothing is wrong with that if that is what the reviewer and the firm want as long as skill and quality levels don't deteriorate, and grow with changing situations. With the latter being adhered to, reviewing becomes a safe, secure and essential job.

However, if the reviewer wants to advance then it is up to the reviewer to do something about it, and be proactive in managing his or her career. From the firm's standpoint, having smart, alert reviewers who are happy in their positions is a great thing for the firm. There is no pressure for advancement other than regular raises and a key position is filled by a reliable person fully conversant with firm systems and procedures.

For the reviewer that wants to advance, they need to become a manager of more than the review work they do – they need to coordinate and integrate procedures with the administartive part of the firm, need to have regular dialogues with the software providers, be on top of new programs and methods such as implementing smart scanners, use of client portals or paperless procedures (which are now all old news, but you get the idea what I mean) or lean processes, have to do more training and probably conduct pre tax season and tax update courses and run a post tax season assessment, and be "in the face" of everyone involved in any way with tax preparation.

Not easy, but the boundaries need to be extended...by the reviewer. It can start very easily with the administrative personnel.

Without coordination with the admin department the work just won't get sent to the client. Admin schedules need to be coordinated with the work flow. For instance, the admin people that usually go home on Saturdays at 1:00 need to stay the last two Saturdays before April 15 to

make sure everything that could be proceessed and go out, gets out –
especially if a 4:00 pick up can be arranged with FedEx or UPS. Even
without a pick up – emails and portals can be used until the last return
that could be processed, is.

I give this job to the MBWRer or one of the reviewers. Further, the
reviewers should make sure all admin procedures are followed such as
filing to the paperless file cabinet, so if a partner gets a call the next day
(yes – some partners do take calls from certain clients on a Sunday) or
early Monday, the return can be accessed.

Leaders that want reviewers to advance will push, but in most firms I've
consulted with, the leaders are content with the reviewers as they are –
it is the reviewers that need to p u s h!

CHAPTER 15:

Reviewers' Last Thing

The reviewer needs to conduct their own top side review before the return gets passed on to be printed (either paper, digital or pdf) and assembled to be sent to the partner to sign and release to the client.

The partner will do their own top side review before signing it – so why shouldn't the reviewer do it first to catch any error that might have slipped through?

Very little effort is needed to compare the return to the previous year looking for big differences.

Rather than this, I find using the Excel tax comparison worksheet to compare the return to last year's return and the projection, if one was done, a highly effective way of reviewing the final results.

The last thing a reviewer should do is to look at every page of the return and make sure nothing jumps out. Many mistakes – sometimes large ones, such as...

- not treating a pension distribution as a tax free rollover,
- not annualizing the penalty on Form 2210,
- not picking up basis for a sale of restricted stock,
- picking up a state tax refund as income where there was no tax benefit the previous year,
- not picking up an AMT credit, or
- not telling a client to set up a SEP for income reported on a Schedule C

...are discovered this way.

It's a form of speed reading and it's a highly effective way that the brain processes information.

CHAPTER 16:

Partner Review When Signing

The return is reviewed once again possibly by the tax partner, but finally by the partner who signs it. The tax projection would be reviewed as well to determine if the return is on target with the projection and information that was given to the client. Notes also should be made then about planning opportunities for the client.

Experienced partners easily uncover many errors by simply looking at the output and comparing it with the previous year's return. The Excel comparison is a tool to assist in this, speeds it up and provides an amazing amount of information to the partner in an instant of time.

Other errors spotted can include incorrect Social Security numbers, addresses, and spelling of clients' names and wrong or old mailing addresses.

Having the preparer look for these types of errors beforehand would:

- raise the quality of the finished product passed on to the reviewer (and partner)
- reduce reviewer's time,
- reduce error correction time,
- reduce total processing and handling time,
- reduce redo's if partner finds an error, and
- would avoid having an upset partner.

Any error that gets through to the partner is the reviewer's error, not the preparer's.

CHAPTER 17:

Post Tax Season Assessment and Follow-up

The Tax Season Assessment should be reviewed twice. At the end of tax season *and* at the beginning. At the end, to review the performance. At the beginning, to set forth expectations. Look this over and consider adopting it as part of your quality control procedures...

☐ Was review time reasonable (less than 25% of preparer time)?

☐ Were review comments excessive based on complexity of return?

☐ Were returns routinely reassigned to preparer or did reviewer or someone else make corrections?

☐ Were returns resubmitted to reviewer within two days of being assigned to make corrections?

☐ Did preparer complete all necessary checklists and worksheets?

☐ Were review comments and diagnostics addressed completely?

☐ Were the reviewers properly trained?

☐ If non-tax managers or partners reviewed returns, did they do a satisfactory job?

☐ Were there any review bottlenecks or with a reviewer that were not cleared up within one day?

☐ Were there delays in needed decisions from partners or managers? [this is important because many times it is the partner that creates a hold-up which then causes last minute crises]

☐ Were review notes evaluated in the aggregate after tax season to uncover repetitive errors?

☐ Were follow up notes for the current year filed properly for easy retrieval next year?

Delays by partners or managers not making decisions in a timely manner are a major cause of delays. Usually when a reviewer is working on a return and they need a decision made they turn to the partner or manager who knows the client best. Any delay in a response will cause multiple touches and certainly delays.

Also, delaying the finalization of the review can be when the preparer is not available to make changes. The partner's delay causes disruption in the system.

Following is a checklist for tax season follow up...

TAX SEASON FOLLOW UP SHEET

Based on issues disclosed by preparer or reviewer

Client_____ Year_____ Date _____

Prepared_____ By_____

Date followed up_____

Comments

_____

_____

_____

_____

Date followed up_____

Comments

_____

_____

_____

Date followed up_____

Comments

_____

_____

_____

_____

Issue(s) discussed

_____

_____

_____

_____

Follow up action

_____

_____

_____

_____

Client comments

_____

_____

_____

_____

Final resolution:

Additional services performed

_____

_____

_____

_____

Future follow up date_____

Client has no interest in corrective or preventative actions _____

Additional Comments

_____

_____

_____

CHAPTER 18:

Ed's Super-Simplified Seven-Step Tax Return Review System

Everything I suggest in here is recommended and should be done. Each firm will use and adopt what they want and what fits into their practice.

Many times I am asked for a quick down and dirty suggested review method so I put the following together. This should not be a substitute for reading the book and considering all my recommendations, but here it is:

1. Reviewer receives a completed tax return ready to be sent to client, with all back up properly indexed on server

2. Reviewer looks at Excel® worksheet for large differences, inconsistent amounts, surprise items, and compares to projection, if one was done, and prior years' amounts

3. If unexpected items or differences from projection, then reviewer would look at preparer notes and reconciliation, and make sure differences are understood and logical

4. Reviewer follows the reviewer's checklist. All items that require reconciliation or comments should have been done by preparer and the reviewer will just have to do a quick once-over

5. Selected items can be spot checked

6. Return should be "locked" in tax program so changes cannot be made after final review

7. Reviewer should look at every page of completed return

APPENDIX

Ed's Excel® Method

Excel® tax comparison worksheets as a review, training, planning, and user-friendly tool

It is not often that a single tool serves multiple, highly essential purposes. The Excel® tax comparison worksheet is such a tool. (Any spreadsheet program can be used. We use Excel and describe it as such, but it is not necessarily an Excel product.)

The worksheet is a simple comparison of the client's current and previous years' tax returns, with some variations that make it easier to review returns, train staff, plan with the client, and give the client a user-friendly summary of their tax return that promotes better meetings and discussions. Please note that the worksheets are not a calculation method but a means of presentation.

Mostly every tax preparation program produces tax comparison schedules with the prior year. The problem with these comparisons is that they cover the categories and totals as they appear on the tax return, and not as the client understands their income, expenses, and tax situation. The Excel® tax comparison worksheets correct these deficiencies.

What it is

The worksheet has columns for the current and last few years. The line items from the tax return are entered on the worksheet with the exception of K-1 components, which are grouped together. Additionally, there is usually an extra column for a projection of the current year. Occasionally we also include the column of the projection for the previous year, for which the return has just been completed, so a comparison can be made of how close the final return came to the projection. The comparison columns also provide a frame of reference and isolate large differences between the projection and actual return amounts, or between the previous and current years.

The K-1 items are grouped to more meaningfully present the client's income and the activity from the entities issuing the K-1. For example, a K-1 with high interest income that is not so grouped would be included with the interest income as it appeared on the tax return and would distort the client's actual personal interest income when they were looking at or analyzing their income for the year. On the other hand, not including it with the other K-1 activities would distort the net income or loss from the entity providing the K-1. In my experience, clients never think of the individual parts of the K-1s; they only center in on the net result.

Illustration: Let's take an example of a client getting a K-1 with $50,000 interest income and a $40,000 business operating loss. The actual income from the entity was $10,000. That is the way the client will relate to that entity. The client could also have $5,000 interest income from bonds and savings accounts. However, their tax return will show $55,000 as interest income (which the client usually won't be able to easily relate to) and a Schedule E $40,000 operating loss (which they also won't easily be able to relate to). The Excel sheet would show $5,000 interest income and $10,000 net income from the entity. Using the Excel sheets makes it easier for the client to understand their financial situation and plan, and for us to advise them. It also makes comparing the client's activities easier when a reviewer or partner reviews the return.

Where applicable, you should provide summaries of the client's interest and dividend income by account or payer with an analysis of taxability by the federal government and each state where client is subject to tax. You can also prepare summaries of rental property and Schedule Cs. This, too, will explain it better for the client, and will make it easier for the reviewer in that they will not have to duplicate certain work processes already done by the preparer.

The Excel file can have lines or an accompanying separate worksheet providing an analysis of tax carry-forwards including Schedule E rental property items, K-1 activities, capital gains, business operating losses, investment interest expense, charity deductions, and alternative minimum tax credit availability.

Some accountants who use these worksheets do not use them for clients for who they do not do projections for, or who do not have K-1s, multiple brokerage or voluminous investment accounts and any property or Schedule Cs, preferring instead to use the two-year comparison from their tax preparation software.

I do not recommend this because I believe that maximum efficiency is attained when as much of the procedures are uniformly applied eliminating "thinking" or deciding when to use. A hurried and harried preparer will always decide not to do something. Having it for everyone also presents a quick bird's eye view on their situation and I have found many situations when this was extremely helpful for a relatively small client.

Also, do not forget the Excel worksheet is a self-checking mechanism. Further, a personal note: I had a planning meeting in the beginning of December with a client that I never needed to do planning with and looked for the Excel sheet on our server. When I could not find it, I ended up printing the first four pages of his prior year's return. At the meeting, a comparison of his W-2 income for the last three years was needed, which was not available easily at that meeting. With the Excel sheet, it would have been a no-brainer since we would have had the info. Note: I spent more time than the original preparer would have spent and I would have had a more efficient meeting.

Using the Excel® worksheets in the review process

The Excel worksheet is an effective review tool. The actual numbers on the final return are entered on the Excel worksheet and compared to the projection for that year, if one was done, and the previous years' actual amounts. The reviewer will also eyeball the prior two or three years' amounts. Comparing each item can be easily done in a matter of a minute or two, or five or ten minutes for involved returns. Any major variances can easily be identified and then researched in the client's documents. Using this method will identify almost every major, material, illogical, or unexpected difference. When I am supervising a preparer, I review the Excel sheet (not the return) for differences and accuracy of the preparation prior to having them hand in the return for the actual review.

Because the preparer is aware of the review procedure with the worksheet, the preparer would be best advised to perform these steps for themselves before handing in the return for review. It is always better for the preparer, rather than the reviewer, to find their errors.

This pre-review process by the preparer also allows them to take a few moments to look at the big picture and reflect on what they did. It is amazing how many of their own errors they find. Also, it gives the preparer a big-picture look at the tax return and client's situation which they lose sight of many times in the effort to "move" the return to the next step.

Using the Excel worksheets also makes it easier to look for and uncover tax or financial planning possibilities for the client. Even if it is too late for planning for the return that was just prepared, or the year that just ended, planning can be recommended for the current or later years. When doing the pre-review of the return by comparing and possibly reconciling it to the projection, don't overlook the opportunity to save the client taxes for the past year by applying for refunds for previous years.

Training

I cannot overemphasize the need for thorough directed training of preparers and reviewers. The importance of training the preparers is to get a better product that will be easier to review and therefore free up the reviewer's mind to look for tax savings opportunities instead of spending most of their time "ticking and tying."

The Excel worksheet is an effective tool that can train the preparer. We said earlier that the preparer should use the Excel worksheet to compare the completed return to the projection and to last year's return and make sure there are no great differences. By completing the Excel worksheet the preparer is virtually forced to make this comparison. If they do not, it will become obvious to the reviewer and will necessitate him or her finding out why the preparer entered numbers on the worksheet without thinking. "Knock knock – is anyone there?"

Any large differences between the prior and current years items should be looked into to make sure no errors were made. Where projections were done the comparison should also be made with the projection. All of this should be explained to the preparer.

Another training tip: Note that many preparers might do a diligent job of preparing the return and tying in all their work, but they neglect to look at the final return they just completed. Experienced reviewers easily uncover many errors by simply looking at the output and comparing it to the previous year's return. Such errors can include Social Security numbers, addresses, and spelling of clients' names. Getting the preparer to do this first would raise the quality of the finished product passed on to the reviewer and would reduce the reviewer's time, the error correction time, and the total processing and handling time. This is not instead of the Excel sheets, but in addition to.

Planning

The planning part of the Excel worksheet is better done when the essential information is presented in an easy to digest bird's eye view. This eliminates time and effort shuffling papers. Even though a projection might be prepared using dedicated projection software or the tax projection feature of your preparation program, the information should also be entered on the Excel sheet. The over 20 pages of output from some programs, including summary sheets, do not show the data in an easy to view manner. Therefore, the summaries should be entered on an Excel spreadsheet. The better the presentation of the information, the more effective and substantive the meeting.

We also prepare Excel spreadsheets for basis and suspended loss calculations, and nonstatutory options and/or incentive stock options. For some clients, we track cash flow information reported on the K-1 schedules.

Cross-selling opportunities

Almost every tax client needs additional services the preparer can provide. The issue becomes not how to approach them with suggestions, but when. Not doing it eliminates an opportunity to better serve the client and to improve your revenue and client relationship.

One way is to keep a follow-up list of advice that you've given to the client at your projection or tax information meetings. Another way is to scan your meeting notes and put them in a folder that you can review after tax season. And yet another method is to collect copies of the Excel tax return summaries that a partner then reviews to determine whether there are additional tax or financial planning opportunities for the client. You can also specifically review all clients with a Schedule C to see if a pension plan is applicable, and if so, call them. Finally, you can suggest opening Keogh, SEP, SIMPLE, or defined benefit plans, or to exercise stock options and triggers in deferred compensation plans where appropriate.

A rebuttal to the skeptics

I have found that most people are reluctant to try the Excel worksheets because:

- It is a new method (Not to me – I have been using it for over a quarter of a century – actually over 40 years).
- It adds time (at the lower levels. It is not good business management to save the time of the lowest level staff at the

expense of the higher levels, or to not try to save the time of the most valuable personnel who cost more and are in much shorter supply).

- The "staff" will resist it with every morsel of strength they have. However, the staff are the ones not handing in high quality work that has been self-reviewed beforehand. And if they did the excellent work expected of them and for which they are being paid for, their pride in their work would make them willing to try new things.

- The partners need to oversee the implementation of the program and cannot permit exceptions. I have found that when training, allowing exceptions effectively destroys the system you are trying to introduce.

- If you were a manufacturer, the cost of a machine, its installation and training would be measured against the future benefits. Do that with this program. It works. Trust me on that!

A last word to skeptics: Have one person try Excel worksheets on the next three returns they work on and then evaluate the overall effectiveness.

The final last word to skeptics, and a challenge: Email me and I'll send you a template; use it to enter your last three years' tax return information, and possibly your projection; then enter your current year information when you complete your return.

If you do not feel this is an effective method, call me and I will be glad to discuss it with you.

Seven Sample Excel® Worksheets

Sample 1. Basic Worksheet (pages 1 and 2). The basic worksheet is prepared for everyone, whether or not we do a projection.

> **Basic Worksheet (page 1).** The first page has a summary of the last few years and a column for the current year's projection. If a projection is not being done for that client, or at that time, this column is omitted. We include this worksheet with the actual final tax return as a multiyear summary.

> **Basic Worksheet (page 2).** The second page has a summary of the tax payments and tax due.

Samples 2 (a) and (b). Interest and Dividends. These schedules show the interest and dividends from various sources and are categorized the way they would be reflected on the tax return.

Sample 3. K-1 Schedule. The items from each K-1 are entered here and categorized. The totals are transferred to page 1 of the Excel sheet. The client will see the summary and has this worksheet with all the details.

Sample 4. Schedule C Multiyear Comparison.

Sample 5. Schedule E Rental Property Multiyear Comparison.

Sample 6. 1099B Reconciliation Worksheet.

Sample 7. Tax Payments Worksheet.

Sample 1. Basic Worksheet (page 1)

T:\123456
HARRY & DAVIDA ORANGE
Tax Comparison
Updated : 12/10/20XX
Status: Joint return

	20TT Actual	20UU Amended	20VV Actual	20WW Actual	20XX Projected	Comments
Salary	63,950	-				
Interest income (non K-1)	8,826	14,602	17,643	11,833	12,000	
Less tax exempt portion	(6,826)	(10,934)	(11,899)	(11,095)	(11,000)	
Dividend income	7,715	13,000	6,820	3,581	4,000	
Taxable state tax refund						
Business income						
Consulting	48,914	44,034	38,320	82,126	86,000	See separate schedule attached
Royalties		137				
Other gains			7			
Capital gains						
Capital loss carryforward from prior year	82,629	44,017	-	(174,266)	(194,001)	
Current year capital gain (loss)			(177,266)	(22,735)		
Capital loss carryforward to next year			174,266	194,001	191,001	
K-1 income						
R.E.Management Company LLC (50%)						
Ordinary income	276,122	309,054	266,012	245,594	230,000	
Interest income	236	1,418	1,613	732	-	
AB Realty (0.52%)						
Rental income	1,716	1,517	1,791	696	1,500	
Interest income	36	58	51	22	-	
CD Realty (1%)						
Rental income	4,703	3,623	3,253	(1,734)	1,500	
Interest income	406	455	281	62	-	
EF Realty (50%)						
Rental income	35,270	6,316	26,971	60,290	78,000	
Interest income	2,157	2,603	1,403	873	-	
GH Associates LLC (50%)						
Ordinary income	2,545	(412)	(4)	(162)	-	
Interest income	2,010	-				
Orange Family FLP (1.5%)						
Rental income	10,213	9,623	10,448	8,671	11,000	
Interest income	416	548	405	137	-	
H & D Properties Corp (100%) (1% of FLP)						
Ordinary Income		(825)	(1,010)			
Rental income		6,415	6,965	5,506	7,000	
Interest income		365	270	91	-	
Adjustments						
One-half of self-employment tax	(6,228)	(10,773)	(10,399)	(11,008)	(11,060)	
SEP contribution	(9,595)	(8,538)	(7,402)	(15,873)	(16,626)	
Adjusted Gross Income	**525,215**	**430,695**	**348,532**	**377,342**	**389,314**	
Itemized deductions						
Medical expenses				18,212	10,801	
Income taxes						
Credit from prior year	3,327	1,518				
Prior balance paid					4,335	
Current year estimates paid by 12/31	10,178	30,370	16,063	15,127	8,255	
Prior year estimate paid January	10,000				10,573	
Adj for refund attrib to current year taxes	(1,493)		(775)	(154)	(279)	
Real estate taxes	19,759	20,194	21,232	22,061	23,000	
Mortgage interest	26,907	28,687	28,923	27,630	26,000	
Points and amortization	1,000					
Contributions - cash	19,360	16,578	19,051	13,776	13,000	
Contributions - noncash		4,500				Any noncash contributions?
Investment interest expense	122	373	101			
Employee business expenses (allowable)	0	-				Any Unreimb K-1 expenses?
Less 3% AGI Floor	(7,494)	(5,486)	(1,886)	(2,105)	-	
Total itemized deductions	85,680	96,734	82,709	94,547	95,685	
Exemptions	4,400	4,532	9,893	9,732	14,600	
Taxable Income	**435,135**	**329,429**	**255,930**	**273,063**	**279,029**	
Federal income tax	107,838	76,958	62,091	67,366	69,231	
SE tax	12,456	21,546	20,798	22,016	22,119	
AMT	11,059	17,378	8,809	12,976	18,779	
Foreign tax credit	(391)	(497)	(96)	(311)		
Total Federal Tax	**130,962**	**115,385**	**91,602**	**102,047**	**110,129**	
New York Income Tax	**33,770**	**25,489**	**20,398**	**24,756**	**26,118**	

Sample 1. Basic Worksheet (page 2)

Schedule of Estimated Tax Payments and Tax Due

	Federal	Federal	Federal	Federal	Federal	
Total tax per above	130,962	115,385	91,602	102,047	110,129	
Penalty & Interest	92	2,764	875	844	1,530	
Overpayment credited	(18,388)	0		(1,005)	0	
Withholding	(14,460)	0				
Estimated tax payments:						
4/15		(15,930)	(15,660)	(14,652)	(12,096)	
6/15	(23,080)	(9,660)	(9,660)	(12,270)	(9,076)	
9/15	(19,872)	(20,358)	(14,004)	(19,490)	(13,770)	
12/31			(19,158)			
1/15	(28,860)	(20,472)	(30,000)	(33,698)	0	
Amount paid with extension	(24,000)	0	(5,000)	(10,000)	0	
Amount paid with original return		(57,400)				
Excise Tax	(60)	0				
Total Payments	(128,660)	(123,820)	(93,482)	(91,115)	(34,942)	
Amount credited to next year		0	1,005	0	0	
Balance Due (Overpayment)	**2,334**	**(5,671)**	**0**	**11,776**	**76,717**	
% of this years tax	98%	107%	102%	89%	32%	
% of last years tax	193%	95%	81%	99%	34%	
	NY	NY	NY	NY	NY	
Total tax per above	33,770	25,489	20,398	24,756	26,118	
Penalty & Interest	86	274	154	279	0	
Overpayment credited	(3,327)			(511)	0	
Withholding	(4,014)					
Estimated tax payments:						
4/15		(3,700)	(3,636)	(3,399)	(2,986)	
6/15	(5,547)	(2,240)	(2,240)	(2,857)	(2,079)	
9/15	(4,631)	(4,945)	(3,245)	(3,360)	(3,190)	
12/31		(4,752)	(6,942)			
1/15	(6,733)			(10,573)	0	
Amount paid with extension	(8,000)	0	(5,000)		0	
Amount paid with original return		(11,857)				
Total Payments	(32,252)	(27,494)	(21,063)	(20,700)	(8,255)	
Amount credited to next year			511	0	0	
Balance Due (Overpayment) 4/15	**1,604**	**(1,731)**	**-**	**4,335**	**17,863**	
% of this years tax	96%	108%	103%	84%	32%	
% of last years tax	151%	81%	83%	101%	33%	

Sample 2 (a). Interest

Interest Income Reconciliation

0   Prepared By: 0
0   Reviewed By: 0

Interest

Payer	Interest Income	U.S. Savings Bonds	Federal Tax Withheld	Investment Expenses	Early Withdrawal Penalty	Tax Exempt Interest	State NonTaxable	State Taxable	Amount Subject to AMT	Foreign Tax Paid	Foreign Country	Schedule A Investment Advisory Fees
Bank and Brokerage Statements												
Subtotal:	-	-	-	-	-	-	-	-	-	-	-	-
K-1's												
Subtotal:	-	-	-	-	-	-	-	-	-	-	-	-
Total	-	-	-	-	-	-	-	-	-	-	-	-

Sample 2 (b). Dividends

Dividend Income Reconciliation

0   Prepared By: 0
0   Reviewed By: 0

Dividends

Payer Name	Ordinary Dividends	Qualified Dividends	Total Capital Gain Distribution	Unrecaptured Section 1250 Gain	Nontaxable Distributions	Federal Tax Withheld	Investment Expenses	State Nontaxable	State Taxable	Amount Subject to AMT	Foreign Tax Paid	Foreign Country	U.S. Bonds - Amount or % in Box 1 (Ordinary Div.)	Cash Liquidation Distribution	Noncash Liquidation Distribution
Bank and Brokerage Statements															
Subtotal:	-	-	-	-	-	-	-	-	-	-	-	-	-	-	-
K-1's															
Subtotal:	-	-	-	-	-	-	-	-	-	-	-	-	-	-	-
Total	-	-	-	-	-	-	-	-	-	-	-	-	-	-	-

Sample 3. K-1 Schedule

Client				20YY Proj	20XX										
Tax summary worksheet - K-1s															
Tax year 20YY															
Prepared:															
					Note: Add columns as necessary based on K-1s client received										
K-1 and Grantor Trust Summary															
Entity	W/P Ref	P/A	ST		Net Effect of K-1's	State Sourc	Income (Loss)	Rental Income	Interest Income	US Interest	Dividend Income	Long-Term Sec.1231	Capital Gain/(Loss)	179 Deduction	Charity
					-										
Total Partnership K-1's					-		-	-	-	-	-	-	-	-	-
Total S-Corp K-1's					-		-	-	-	-	-	-	-	-	-
					-										
					-										
					-										
					-										
					-										
Total Grantor Trust Income									-	-	-	-	-		-
Total K-1 and Grantor Trust Income					-		-	-	-	-	-	-	-	-	-
							179 expense					line12 of Sch D			
Ordinary K-1 Income															
1231 Gain															
Prior Disallowed Passive Losses															
Prior Disall. Pub Tr Ptsp Passive Losses															
Disallowed Passive Losses												-			
Disallowed Pub Tr Ptship Passive Losses												Sch D line 11			
Pass Through Income (Loss)															
							Form 1040, Line 17					Form 1040, Line 14			

Sample 4. Schedule C Multiyear Comparison

Client Name_____

Tax summary worksheet

Tax year:

Prepared:

Schedule C

Business name:_____

	20UU	20VV	20WW	20XX
Revenues				
Cost of sales				
Gross profit				
Advertising				
Auto expenses				
Commissions				
Depreciation				
Insurance				
Legal and professional services				
Office expenses				
Rent				
Auto lease				
Repairs and maintenance				
Supplies				
Licenses				
Travel				
Meals				
Less nondeductible meals				
Utilities				
Other expenses				
Fed Ex and Courier				
Conventions				
Website maintenance				
Outside services				
Total expenses				
Net income				

Sample 5. Schedule E Rental Property Multiyear Comparison

Client Name_____			
Tax summary worksheet			
Tax year:			
Prepared:			
Schedule E			
Property address:_____			
	20UU	**20VV**	**20WW**	**20XX**
Rent income				
Advertising				
Cleaning and maintenance				
Commissions				
Insurance				
Legal and professional fees				
Mortgage interest				
Repairs				
Supplies				
Taxes				
Utilities				
Other				
Inspection fees				
Snow removal				
Depreciation				
Total expenses				
Net income				

Sample 6. 1099B Reconciliation Worksheet

RECONCILIATION OF FORMS 1099-B AND 1099-S	
Client Name:	
Year:	
Proceeds From Stocks, Bonds, Etc., And Real Estate Sales:	
Name of Broker	**Amount**
Total	$ -
Total Sales Price Amounts Reported On Schedule D:	
Line	**Amount**
3	
10	
Total	$ -

NOTE:
If the total reported on Schedule D is less than the total amount reported on Forms 1099, attach a statement to the tax return explaining the difference or note the difference below

Sample 7. Tax Payments Worksheet

			STATE INCOME TAX DEDUCTION				
			FEDERAL & STATE TAX PAYMENTS				
	Client:				Year:		
		Federal	NJ	NYS	NYC	SUI/SDI	Other
Withholdings:							
Withholdings per W-2's:							
Employer:							
Other Withholdings (Int., Div., 1099's, K-1's, Excess FICA and SUI/SDI, etc.):							
Source:							
NJ Excess SUI/SDI			-				
Total Withholdings		-	-	-	-	-	-
Estimated tax payments for _____ :							
Credit applied from prior year return:							
(if did not itemized in prior year calculate if should be picked up as income)							
4/15/20XX							
6/15/20XX							
9/15/20XX							
12/31/20XX							
1/15/20XY							
Total Estimated Tax Payments		-	-	-	-	-	-
Total W/H, Estimates & Ext Pymts		-	-	-	-	-	-
Additional payments							
4th Qtr. 20WW Est. pd. In Jan. 20XX						.	
Balance Due for 'WW (Pd. In 'XX)							
WW State Refund Attrib to Taxes Paid in XX							
Other Payments (explain)							
Less: 4th Qtr. 'WW pd Jan. 'YY			-	-	-	-	-
Less: Extension Pmt. Pd. In 'YY			-	-	-	-	-
Total Deduction on Federal Return			-	-	-	-	-
Grand Total Deduction on Federal Return of all State Taxes			-				
Were the estimated tax payments and extension payments verified with cancelled checks? Yes/No							
If answer to above question is NO how were payments verified? Explain							

Answers to the 10-Question Reviewer Qualification Test

1. It can be opened through the latest due date, including extensions for the previous year's tax return.

2. The date the first or original lot of stocks was purchased.

3. Voluntary payments to an ex-spouse are not deductible as alimony.

4. Pre-1987 recaptured depreciation on real estate is taxed at ordinary income rates; 1987 or later recaptured depreciation on real estate is taxed, for 2014 tax reporting, at a top capital gains rate of 25% and might be an additional 3.8% for net investment income.

5. When the income or deductions are earned erratically, bunched or not received or paid equally during the year, and it results in a lower or no 2210 penalty.

6. The gains are taxed as 60% long-term capital gains and 40% short-term capital gains regardless of holding period.

7. The client should consider donating appreciated long-term owned securities. The client would get a charitable deduction for the fair market value of the securities and not have to report the capital gain income.

8. The employer is required to report the entire gain as wages on the employee's Form W-2. I would use $8,100. However, the technically correct answer is that the cost should be the fair market value on the date vested, before deduction for the broker's commission. A practical solution on small transactions is to use the net proceeds.

9. To consider exercising as much of the ISOs as the client can to the point where the AMT would kick in.

10. 5.33%. Divide 4% by 75% (1 − 25%).

10 More Issues That You Can Test

(Depending On The Nature Of Your Practice)

1. Section 1231 losses

2. Section 1245 and 1250 recapture

3. 1244 losses

4. 754 step up

5. Collectible capital gains

6. Contributions of art that is immediately resold by the charity

7. Disclosure thresholds for non-cash charity

8. How charity expense on a Schedule C business is reported

9. Basis of Roth IRA that is terminated early

10. Section 83(b) elections

More from Ed Mendlowitz

More publications by Ed Mendlowitz from CPA Trendlines are available at cpaclick.com/shopcpa:

- Tax Season Opportunity Guide
- How to Increase Your Billing Rates
- The 30:30 Training Method
- 101 Questions and Answers for Managing a Tax and Accounting Practice

Ed Mendlowitz is a regular contributor to CPA Trendlines at cpatrendlines.com and he blogs at partners-network.com. He welcomes reader questions and comments, and can be reached by email at emendlowitz@withum.com, or by phone at (732) 964-9329.

More from CPA Trendlines

at cpaclick.com/shopcpa

- Professional Services Marketing 3.0, by Bruce W. Marcus
- How To Bring in New Partners
- The Annual Rosenberg MAP Survey
- Creating The Effective Partnership: Two-Volume Package
  - o Leadership At Its Strongest
  - o How to Engage Partners in the Firm's Future
- How to Negotiate a CPA Firm Merger
- CPA Firm Succession Planning: A Perfect Storm
- CPA Firm Management & Governance
- The Client Service Idea Book
- Accounting Marketing 101 for Partners
- The Accountant's (Bad) Joke Book
- How CPA Firms Work: The Business of Public Accounting
- What Really Makes CPA Firms Profitable
- Strategic Planning and Goal Setting for Results
- Guide to Planning the Firm Retreat
- How to Operate a Compensation Committee
- Effective Partner Relations and Communications
- The Idea Book for Accounting Firm Hiring Managers
- The Idea Book for Career Planning in Accounting

CPA Trendlines Research is the profession' leading source of actionable business intelligence for the tax, accounting and finance community.

Join at GoProCPA.com.

36697812R00087

Made in the USA
Charleston, SC
16 December 2014